Why things don't work
TRAIN

www.raintreepublishers.co.uk
Visit our website to find out more information about Raintree books.

To order:
☎ Phone 44 (0) 1865 888112
🖹 Send a fax to 44 (0) 1865 314091
💻 Visit the Raintree bookshop at www.raintreepublishers.co.uk to browse
   our catalogue and order online.

Why things don't work TRAIN
was produced by

David West 🧍🧍 Children's Books
7 Princeton Court
55 Felsham Road
London SW15 1AZ

Editor: Dominique Crowley
Consultant: David T. Wright

First published in Great Britain by
Raintree, Halley Court, Jordan Hill, Oxford OX2 8EJ, part of
Harcourt Education. Raintree is a registered trademark of Harcourt
Education Ltd.

Copyright © 2007 David West Children's Books

13 digit ISBN: 978 1 4062 0554 1

11 10 09 08 07
10 9 8 7 6 5 4 3 2 1

British Library Cataloguing in Publication Data

West, David
  Train. - (Why things don't work)
  1.Locomotives - Maintenance and repair - Comic books,
  strips, etc. - Juvenile literature 2.Railroads - Trains -
  Comic books, strips, etc. - Juvenile literature
  I.Title
  625.2'6'0288

Printed and bound in China

Why things don't work

TRAIN

by David West

Contents

6 GRANDMA'S TRAINS

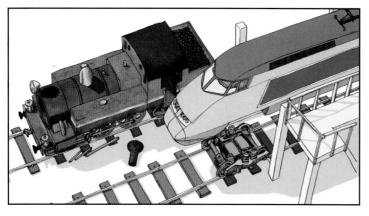

8 TANK ENGINE

10 HOW A STEAM ENGINE WORKS

12 MAKING STEAM

14 THE PISTONS

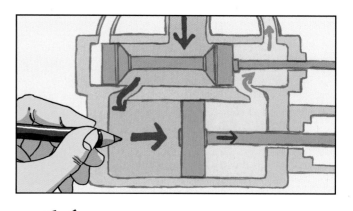

16 TURNING THE WHEELS

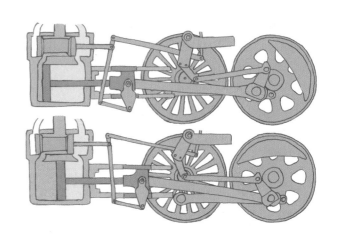

18 FIXING AND FINISHING

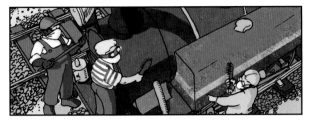

20 BUILDING UP STEAM

22 DRIVING A STEAM TRAIN

24 HIGH-SPEED ELECTRIC TRAIN

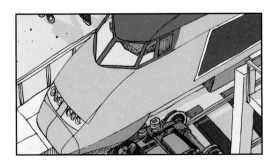

26 PANTOGRAPH, TRANSFORMER, AND COMPUTER

28 THE TRAIN MUSEUM

30 PARTS OF A STEAM TRAIN

31 GLOSSARY
32 INDEX

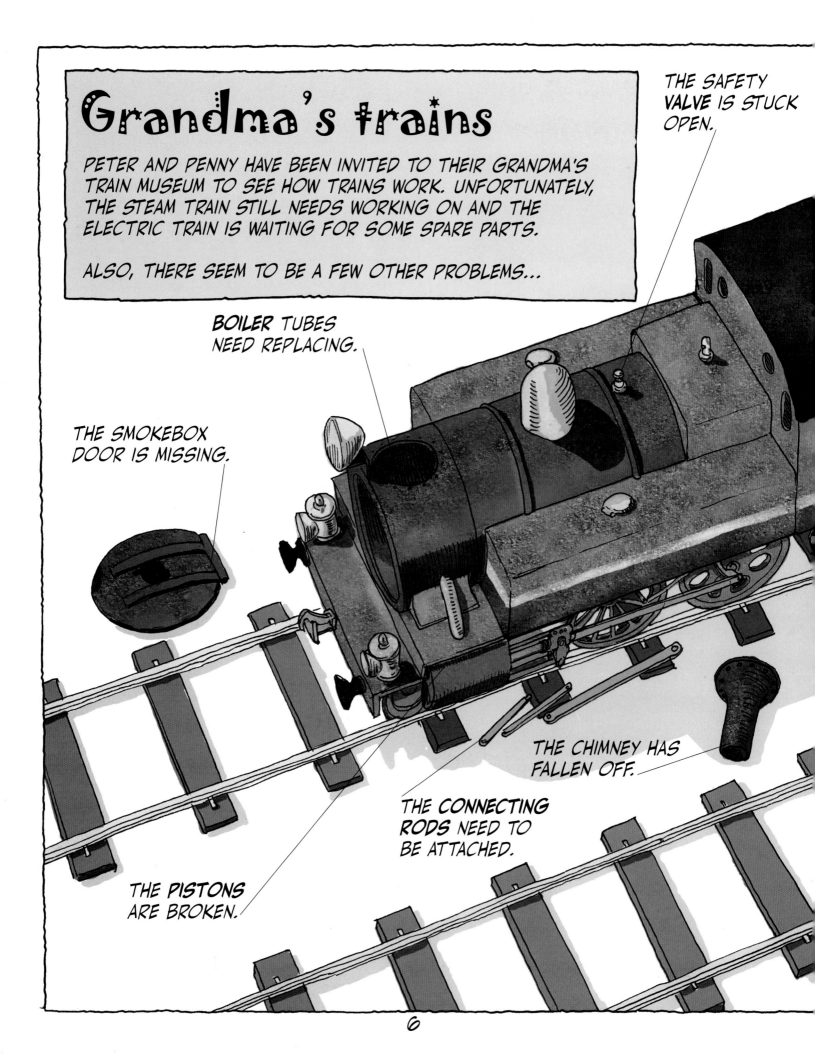

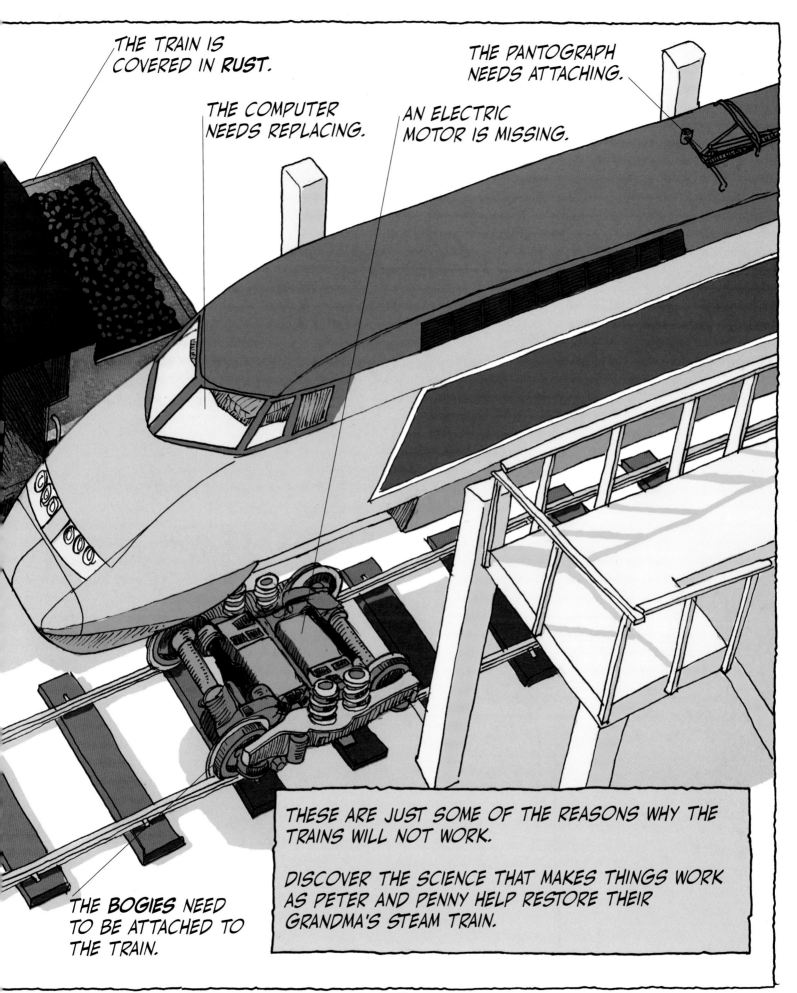

THE TRAIN IS COVERED IN **RUST**.

THE COMPUTER NEEDS REPLACING.

AN ELECTRIC MOTOR IS MISSING.

THE PANTOGRAPH NEEDS ATTACHING.

THE **BOGIES** NEED TO BE ATTACHED TO THE TRAIN.

THESE ARE JUST SOME OF THE REASONS WHY THE TRAINS WILL NOT WORK.

DISCOVER THE SCIENCE THAT MAKES THINGS WORK AS PETER AND PENNY HELP RESTORE THEIR GRANDMA'S STEAM TRAIN.

PETER AND PENNY ARRIVE AT GRANDMA'S TRAIN MUSEUM.

WOW! THIS PLACE IS AMAZING.

THERE'S GRANDMA LIZZIE.

OVER HERE, KIDS.

YOU'VE ARRIVED JUST IN TIME TO HELP WITH MY TANK ENGINE.

LET'S PUT YOUR BAGS IN THE STATION HOUSE.

WHY IS YOUR TRAIN CALLED A TANK ENGINE, GRANDMA?

BECAUSE IT'S GOT WATER TANKS ON THE SIDE OF THE ENGINE.

DOES THE WATER KEEP IT COOL?

NO. YOU NEED LOTS OF WATER TO MAKE THIS ENGINE RUN.

WHAT DO YOU GET WHEN YOU HEAT WATER?

STEAM?

REEEBEP

STEAM. THAT'S RIGHT. THIS TRAIN USES A STEAM ENGINE TO RUN IT.

HOW DOES THE TRAIN MAKE THE STEAM?

FOLLOW ME AND I'LL SHOW YOU.

THAT LONG CYLINDER IS THE BOILER.

THIS IS THE SMOKEBOX. BEHIND IT IS THE BOILER'S WATER AND TUBES.

WHAT ARE ALL THOSE HOLES?

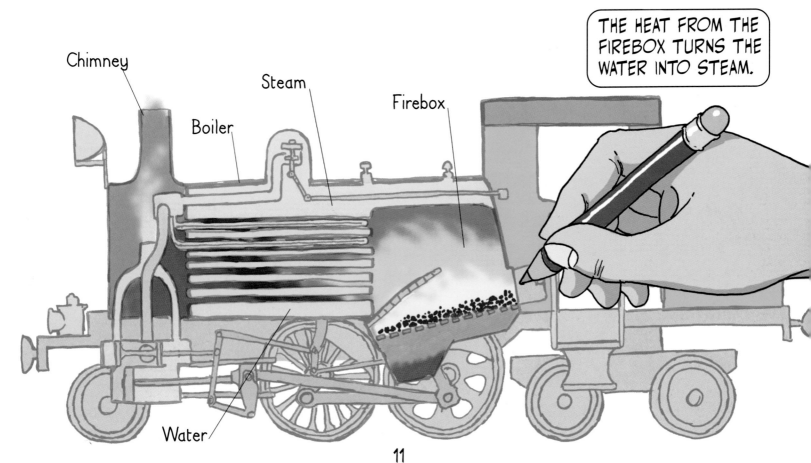

Chimney

Boiler

Steam

Firebox

Water

AS THE WATER TURNS TO STEAM, IT BUILDS UP PRESSURE.

THIS IS BECAUSE STEAM (A GAS) TAKES UP MORE SPACE THAN WATER (A LIQUID).

Steam

Boiling water (100°C)

Heat

BUT THE STEAM IS NOT ALLOWED TO EXPAND UNTIL IT HAS BUILT UP ENOUGH PRESSURE. THEN IT HAS THE POWER TO MOVE THINGS, JUST LIKE THE LID OFF A SAUCEPAN.

Steam

Boiling water

Heat

THIS GAUGE, HERE, SHOWS THE PRESSURE. WHEN THE STEAM GETS TO A HIGH ENOUGH PRESSURE, IT CAN BE PIPED TO THE PISTONS.

YOU CAN SEE THE PISTONS ARE AT THE FRONT. THEY ARE ON EACH SIDE OF THE TRAIN.

AS YOU CAN SEE, THERE ARE TWO PISTONS IN EACH **CYLINDER** CASING.

HOW DO THEY WORK?

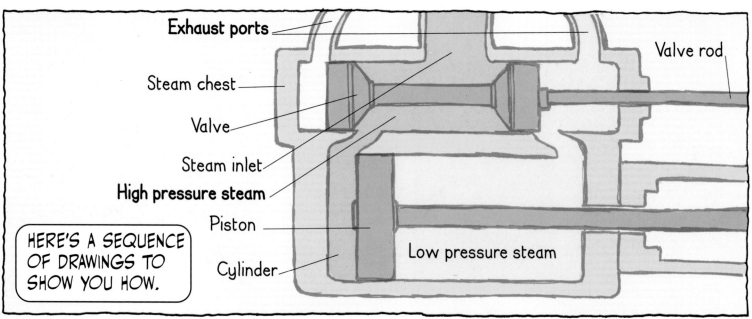

Exhaust ports

Valve rod

Steam chest

Valve

Steam inlet

High pressure steam

Piston

Cylinder

Low pressure steam

HERE'S A SEQUENCE OF DRAWINGS TO SHOW YOU HOW.

HIGH PRESSURE STEAM FROM THE BOILER ENTERS THE CYLINDER THROUGH THE INLET. AS IT EXPANDS IT PUSHES THE PISTON.

WHEN THE PISTON REACHES THE END OF THE CYLINDER, THE VALVE OPENS UP THE EXHAUST PORT. THIS LETS OUT THE STEAM.

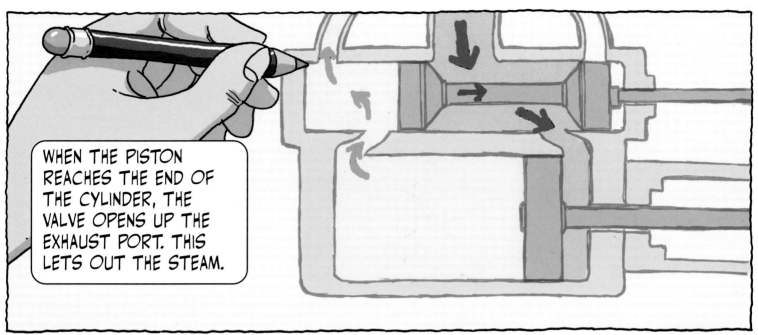

THE VALVE ALSO ALLOWS HIGH PRESSURE STEAM TO ENTER FROM THE RIGHT. THIS PUSHES THE PISTON TO THE OTHER END OF THE CYLINDER.

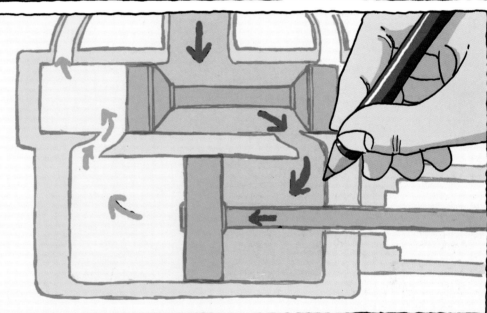

WHEN THE PISTON REACHES THE END OF THE CYLINDER, THE VALVE OPENS UP THE EXHAUST PORT ON THE OTHER SIDE TO ALLOW THE EXPANDED STEAM OUT. THE WHOLE PROCESS IS READY TO START AGAIN.

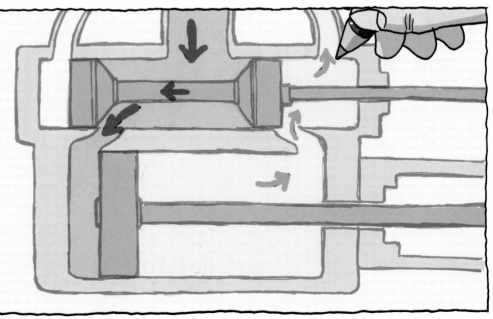

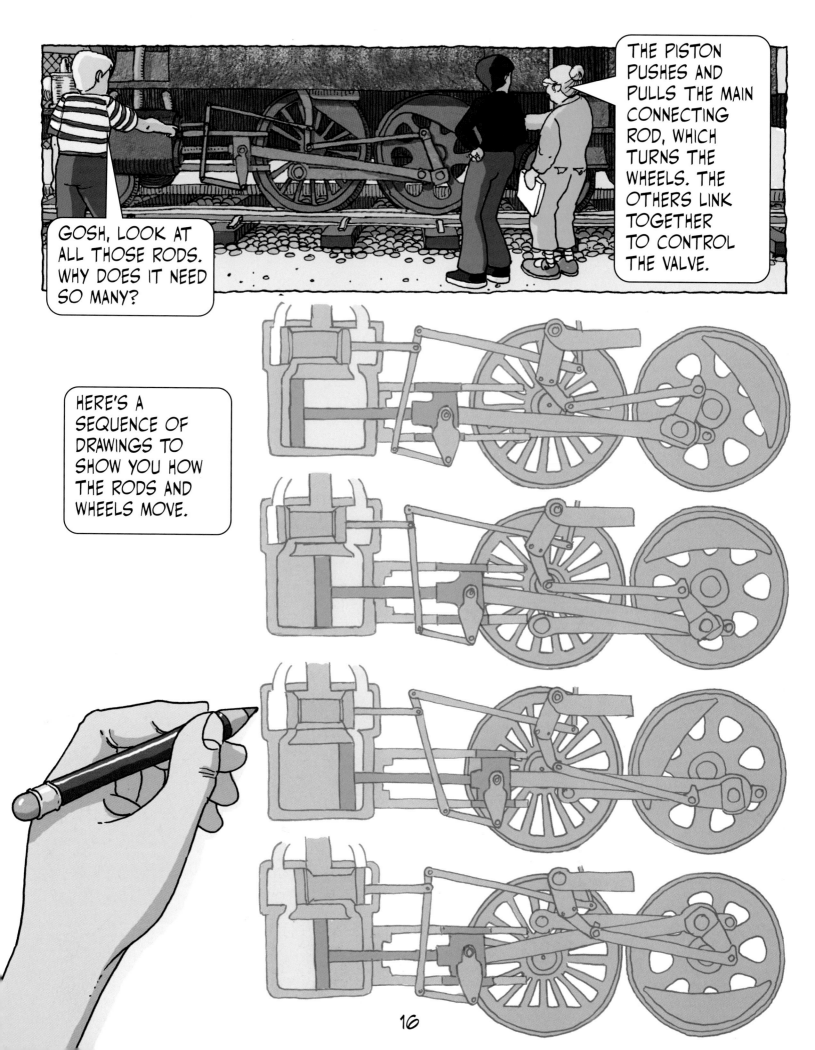

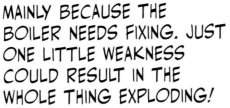

WHY DOESN'T THE TRAIN WORK, GRANDMA?

MAINLY BECAUSE THE BOILER NEEDS FIXING. JUST ONE LITTLE WEAKNESS COULD RESULT IN THE WHOLE THING EXPLODING!

EVEN WHEN THIS TRAIN WAS RUNNING IN THE FIRST HALF OF THE TWENTIETH CENTURY, IT WOULD NEED TO HAVE THE BOILER REPAIRED EVERY FIVE YEARS.

WE'VE NEARLY FINISHED, THOUGH.

WHAT ARE THOSE PIPES FOR?

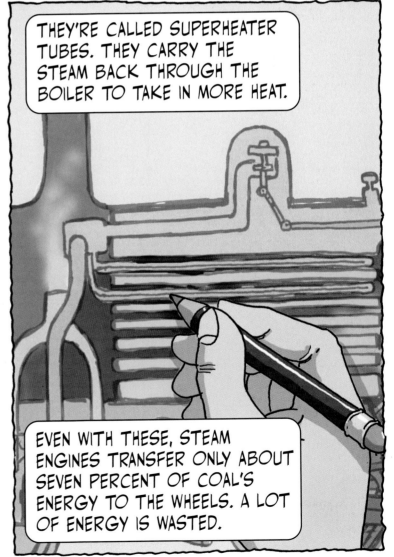

THEY'RE CALLED SUPERHEATER TUBES. THEY CARRY THE STEAM BACK THROUGH THE BOILER TO TAKE IN MORE HEAT.

EVEN WITH THESE, STEAM ENGINES TRANSFER ONLY ABOUT SEVEN PERCENT OF COAL'S ENERGY TO THE WHEELS. A LOT OF ENERGY IS WASTED.

WHAT IS THIS PIPE, HERE?

THAT'S WHERE THE SPENT STEAM FROM THE PISTONS' EXHAUST PORT COMES OUT.

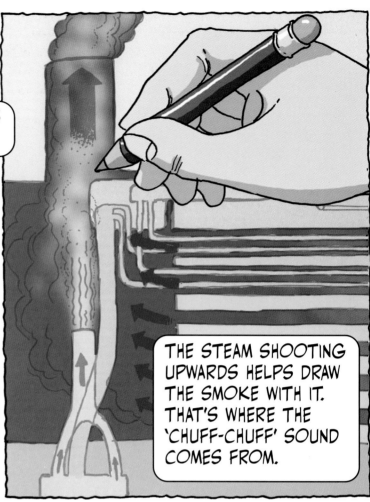

THE STEAM SHOOTING UPWARDS HELPS DRAW THE SMOKE WITH IT. THAT'S WHERE THE 'CHUFF-CHUFF' SOUND COMES FROM.

BY THE END OF THE WEEK, THE TANK ENGINE WAS FINISHED.

THE BOILER HAD BEEN COMPLETELY OVERHAULED.

THE PISTONS HAD BEEN CLEANED AND PUT BACK TOGETHER.

THE SMOKEBOX DOOR HAD BEEN FIXED BACK ON.

THE CHIMNEY HAD BEEN FITTED.

AND ALL THE RODS HAD BEEN OILED AND PUT BACK ON.

FINALLY, WE CLEANED THE WHOLE TRAIN OF RUST...

AND REPAINTED IT.

WHERE DOES RUST COME FROM?

IT'S A CHEMICAL REACTION CALLED **OXIDIZATION**, WHEN OXYGEN IN THE DAMP AIR REACTS WITH THE IRON.

PAINTING THE METAL HELPS PROTECT IT FROM RUSTING.

THAT'S SORTED IT OUT.

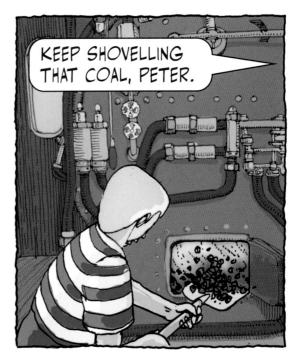

KEEP SHOVELLING THAT COAL, PETER.

LOOK. THE PRESSURE GAUGE SHOWS WE HAVE ENOUGH PRESSURE TO START.

OK, PENNY, RELEASE THAT BRAKE LEVER.

PETER, PULL THE **THROTTLE LEVER**, THERE.

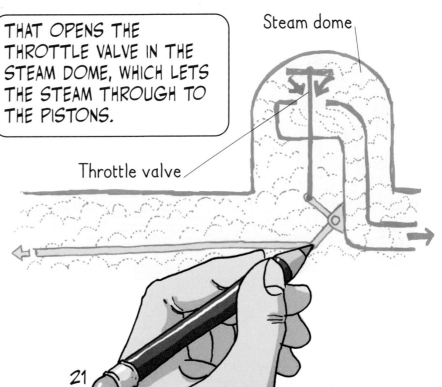

THAT OPENS THE THROTTLE VALVE IN THE STEAM DOME, WHICH LETS THE STEAM THROUGH TO THE PISTONS.

Steam dome

Throttle valve

21

22

HALF AN HOUR LATER...

WE NEED TO STOP NOW AND HEAD BACK.

HOW DO WE TURN ROUND?

CRANK

WE DON'T NEED TO. WE JUST REVERSE THE WHEELS BY PULLING ON THAT LEVER.

THE ENGINE STARTED GOING BACKWARDS.

BACK AT THE TRAIN MUSEUM'S STATION...

THAT WAS COOL!

IF YOU THINK THAT WAS COOL, COME AND SEE MY LATEST ADDITION.

WOW! WHAT IS IT?

IT'S A FRENCH HIGH-SPEED ELECTRIC TRAIN, CALLED A TGV.

WE'RE JUST FINISHING REPAIRING IT.

WHERE'S THE ENGINE?

IT DOESN'T HAVE AN ENGINE LIKE THE STEAM TRAIN.

EACH PAIR OF WHEELS HAS AN ELECTRIC MOTOR.

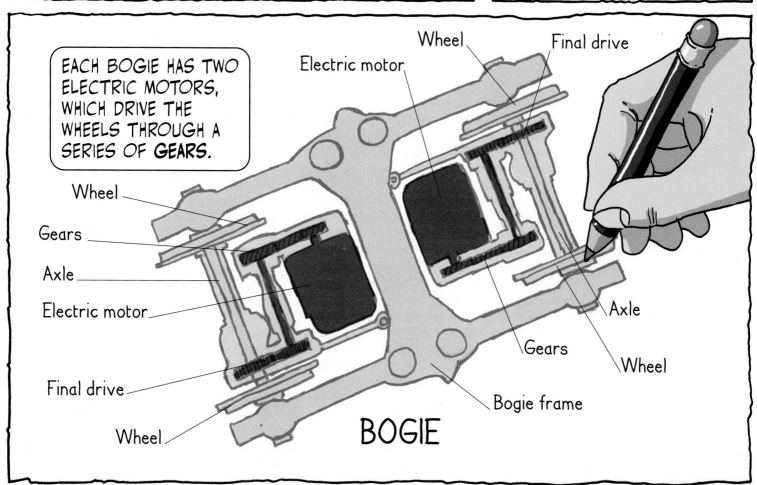

EACH BOGIE HAS TWO ELECTRIC MOTORS, WHICH DRIVE THE WHEELS THROUGH A SERIES OF **GEARS**.

Wheel

Electric motor

Final drive

Wheel

Gears

Axle

Electric motor

Final drive

Wheel

Axle

Gears

Wheel

Bogie frame

BOGIE

HOW DO ELECTRIC MOTORS WORK?

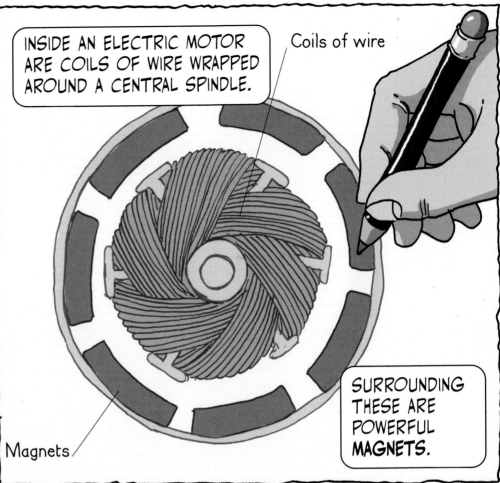

INSIDE AN ELECTRIC MOTOR ARE COILS OF WIRE WRAPPED AROUND A CENTRAL SPINDLE.

Coils of wire

Magnets

SURROUNDING THESE ARE POWERFUL **MAGNETS.**

WHEN ELECTRICITY PASSES THROUGH THE COILS OF WIRE, THEY CREATE A MAGNETIC FIELD OPPOSITE TO THOSE OF THE MAGNETS.

Opposite poles attract. Similar poles **repel.**

S N   S N
S N   N S

THIS MAKES THE COILS OF WIRE **ROTATE,** WHICH CREATES A STRONG TURNING FORCE.

S
N

N

S

WHERE DOES THE TRAIN GET ITS ELECTRICITY FROM?

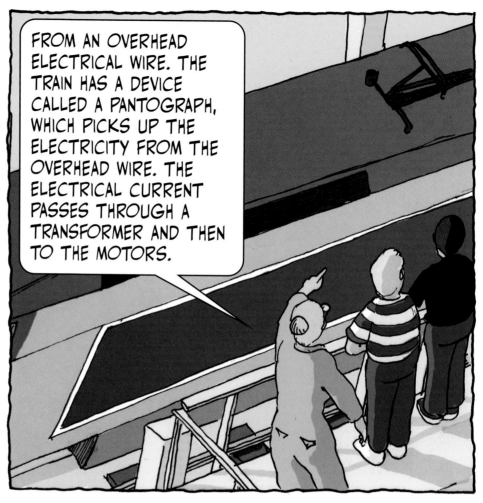

FROM AN OVERHEAD ELECTRICAL WIRE. THE TRAIN HAS A DEVICE CALLED A PANTOGRAPH, WHICH PICKS UP THE ELECTRICITY FROM THE OVERHEAD WIRE. THE ELECTRICAL CURRENT PASSES THROUGH A TRANSFORMER AND THEN TO THE MOTORS.

WHAT'S A TRANSFORMER?

ELECTRICITY IN THE OVERHEAD WIRE IS AT A VERY HIGH VOLTAGE. THE MOTORS USE A LOWER VOLTAGE. THE TRAIN HAS A TRANSFORMER TO CHANGE THE VOLTAGE SO THE MOTORS CAN USE IT. THIS DIAGRAM SHOWS HOW A TRANSFORMER WORKS.

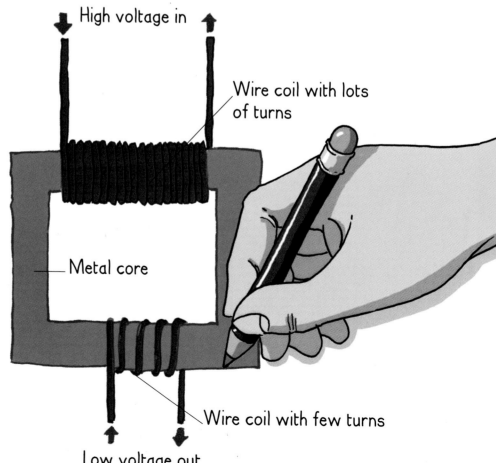

High voltage in

Wire coil with lots of turns

Metal core

Wire coil with few turns

Low voltage out

WHEN WILL YOU HAVE IT WORKING?

VERY SOON. WE'RE JUST WAITING FOR A NEW COMPUTER.

WHY DOES IT NEED A COMPUTER?

ALL THE DIFFERENT SYSTEMS, FROM BRAKES TO ELECTRICAL SUPPLY, NEED TO BE MONITORED AND CONTROLLED. THE **COMPUTER** DOES THIS, SO THE DRIVER CAN CONCENTRATE ON DRIVING THE TRAIN.

27

THE NEXT DAY PETER AND PENNY LOOKED AROUND THE TRAIN MUSEUM.

THIS IS A **REPLICA** OF THE FIRST EVER STEAM TRAIN. IT WAS BUILT BY TREVITHICK IN 1803.

THIS ONE HAS A DEVICE ON THE FRONT CALLED A COW CATCHER.

LOOK AT THIS PICTURE OF BIG BOY. THIS WAS THE BIGGEST STEAM TRAIN EVER BUILT.

THIS IS THE MALLARD, BUILT IN 1938, WHICH STILL HOLDS THE RECORD FOR THE FASTEST STEAM TRAIN AT TWO HUNDRED AND TWO KILOMETRES PER HOUR.

HERE'S A PICTURE OF THE FASTEST ELECTRIC TRAIN. IT'S A JAPANESE BULLET TRAIN. IT'S GOT AIR BRAKES THAT LOOK LIKE EARS.

HERE'S A PICTURE OF A TRAIN THAT HOVERS ON MAGNETS! IT'S CALLED A MAGLEV TRAIN.

FINALLY IT WAS TIME TO GO. GRANDMA DROPPED PETER AND PENNY AT THE TRAIN STATION.

THANKS FOR HELPING ME OUT, KIDS. I'LL LET YOU KNOW WHEN THE TGV IS READY.

LOOK! IT'S THE SAME TRAIN AS GRANDMA'S!

29

Parts of a steam train

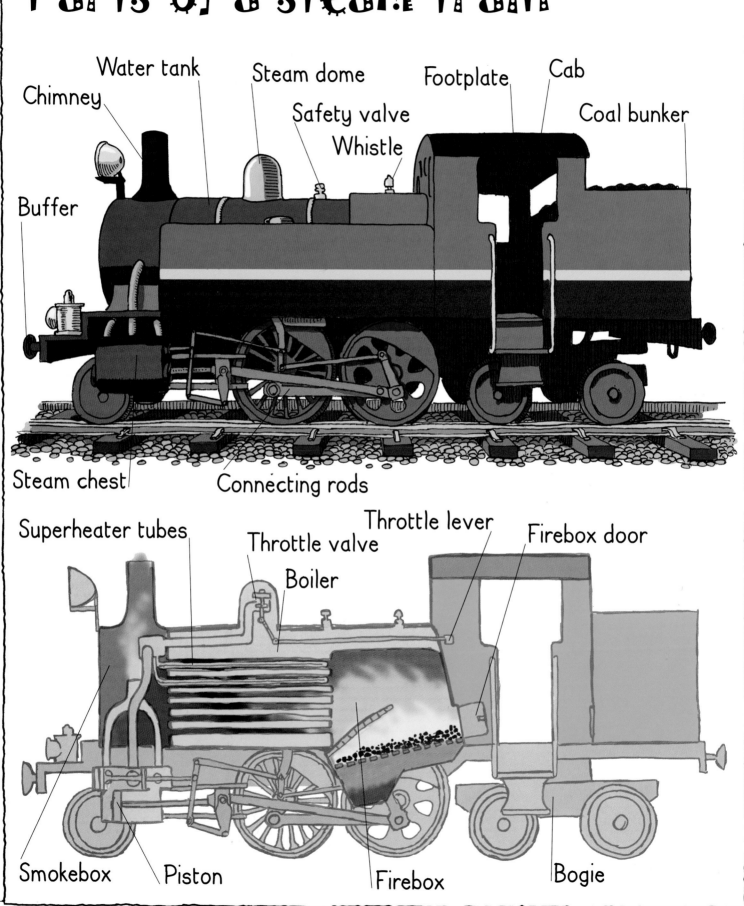

Chimney

Water tank

Steam dome

Safety valve

Whistle

Footplate

Cab

Coal bunker

Buffer

Steam chest

Connecting rods

Superheater tubes

Throttle valve

Throttle lever

Firebox door

Boiler

Smokebox

Piston

Firebox

Bogie

Glossary

BOGIE
FRAME WITH FOUR WHEELS THAT
SUPPORTS THE TRAIN

BOILER
METAL CONTAINER HOLDING WATER THAT
IS TURNED INTO STEAM

COAL BUNKER
PLACE WHERE THE COAL IS STORED

COMPUTER
AN ELECTRONIC DEVICE THAT CAN BE
PROGRAMMED TO CONTROL THE VARIOUS
WORKINGS OF A MACHINE.

CONNECTING RODS
THE METAL RODS ATTACHED TO THE
PISTONS AND THE WHEELS, WHICH TURN
THE WHEELS

CYLINDER
THE METAL SLEEVE INSIDE WHICH A
PISTON MOVES

EXHAUST PORT
THE HOLES IN THE STEAM CHEST
THROUGH WHICH THE EXPANDED
STEAM EXITS

FIREBOX
THE PLACE, INSIDE A STEAM TRAIN, WHERE
THE COAL IS BURNT

GEARS
A SET OF WHEELS THAT TRANSFER
POWER. THE WHEELS HAVE TEETH ON
THEIR RIM, WHICH ALLOWS THEM TO
GRIP EACH OTHER.

HIGH PRESSURE STEAM
STEAM THAT IS VERY HOT AND HAS NOT
BEEN ALLOWED TO EXPAND

MAGNET
A PIECE OF METAL, USUALLY IRON, WHICH
HAS A MAGNETIC FIELD WITH NORTH AND
SOUTH POLES

OXIDIZATION
THE PROCESS OF RUSTING, WHEN A
METAL, SUCH AS IRON, COMBINES WITH
OXYGEN IN A DAMP ATMOSPHERE

PISTON
A SOLID CYLINDER THAT MOVES TO AND
FRO INSIDE ANOTHER, HOLLOW CYLINDER

REPEL
TO FORCE AWAY

REPLICA
A COPY

ROTATE
TURN

RUST
THE RESULT OF OXYDIZATION

THROTTLE LEVER
THE CONTROL, WHICH MAKES THE TRAIN
GO FASTER OR SLOWER

VALVE
A DEVICE THAT OPENS AND CLOSES,
ALLOWING A GAS OR LIQUID THROUGH AN
OPENING – USUALLY ONLY ONE WAY

Index

A

AXLE 24

B

BIG BOY 28
BOGIE 7, 24, 30
BOGIE FRAME 24
BOILER 6, 10, 11, 14, 17, 18, 30
BRAKE LEVER 21
BUFFER 30
BULLET TRAIN 29

C

CAB 30
CHIMNEY 6, 10, 11, 20, 30
COAL 12, 17, 20, 21, 30
COAL BUNKER 12, 30
COMPUTER 7, 27
CONNECTING RODS 6, 30
COW CATCHER 28
CYLINDER 12, 14, 15

E

ELECTRICAL WIRE 26
ELECTRICITY 25, 26
ELECTRIC MOTOR 7, 24, 25
ELECTRIC TRAIN 6-7, 24-29
EXHAUST PORTS 14

F

FINAL DRIVE 24
FIREBOX 11, 12, 30
FIREBOX DOOR 12, 30
FOOTPLATE 20, 30

G

GEARS 24

M

MAGLEV 29
MAGNETS 25, 29
MALLARD 29

O

OXIDIZATION 19

P

PANTOGRAPH 7, 26
PISTON 6, 13, 14, 15, 16, 18, 21, 30
PRESSURE 13, 14, 15, 20, 21

R

REPLICA 28
REVERSING 23
RUST 7, 19

S

SAFETY VALVE 6, 20, 30
SMOKEBOX 6, 10, 19, 30
STATION HOUSE 8
STEAM 9, 10, 11, 13, 14, 15, 17, 20, 21, 22
STEAM CHEST 14, 30
STEAM DOME 21, 30
STEAM INLET 14
STEAM TRAIN 6-23
SUPERHEATER TUBES 17, 30

T

TANK ENGINE 8, 9, 18
TGV 23, 39
THROTTLE LEVER 21, 30
THROTTLE VALVE 21, 30
TRAIN MUSEUM 6, 8, 23, 28

TRANSFORMER 26

V

VALVE 6, 14, 15, 16, 20, 31, 30
VALVE ROD 14
VOLTAGE 26

W

WATER TANK 9, 10, 30
WHEEL 16, 17, 21, 24
WHISTLE 22, 30
WIRE COILS 25, 26